THE GOD WHO IS NEAR

Practicing the Presence of God

a guide for everyday life

BROTHER LAWRENCE

DENNIS LOGAN

The God Who Is Near:
Practicing the Presence of God —
A Guide for Everyday Life
Brother Lawrence & Dennis Logan

© 2025 Penemue Media. All rights reserved.

This edition includes modern commentary, spiritual reflections, appendices, glossary, and supplementary material by **Dennis Logan**.

Original text of *The Practice of the Presence of God* is in the public domain.

No part of this book may be reproduced, stored in a retrieval system, or transmitted in any form or by any means—electronic, mechanical, photocopying, recording, or otherwise—without the prior written permission of the publisher, except in the case of brief quotations used in critical articles or reviews.

Published by **Penemue Media**
Richmond, Virginia, USA

Printed in the United States of America

ISBN: 978-1-964297-23-1

Book design, typesetting, and editorial material by **Dennis Logan**. Cover design by **Dennis Logan**, with assistance from AI-generated imagery.

Scripture quotations, if included, are from public domain translations unless otherwise noted.

This book is not intended to replace professional spiritual, psychological, or medical guidance. The reflections and practices offered herein are for devotional and educational purposes.

2025

EDITORIAL PREFACE

There are books we study, and there are books that study us. *The Practice of the Presence of God* belongs to the second kind.

Across centuries, Brother Lawrence has spoken with a voice that is neither loud nor insistent. Instead, he invites the reader into a way of life shaped not by performance but by awareness—a steady turning of the heart toward the God who is already near. His wisdom is simple enough for a beginner and deep enough for a mystic. And it remains surprisingly necessary in a world overflowing with hurry, noise, and distraction.

This modern guide was created not to improve Brother Lawrence, but to support the reader who wishes to walk with him. My role is not that of a commentator standing over the text, but a fellow pilgrim standing beside you. The reflections, appendices, and practices included here are offered gently—tools for everyday life, not burdens for the soul. You may use them as steps, or as resting places, or set them aside when your heart needs only silence.

What has always moved me about Brother Lawrence is his humility. He did not seek to be a teacher, yet he became one. He did not intend to write a classic, yet one grew from his conversations. He did not claim spiritual brilliance, yet he learned the rare art of discovering God in the ordinary. His way was not dramatic; it was faithful. And that faithfulness created a flame that still warms us.

This edition is meant to bring that flame a little closer to the modern reader—to illuminate the path without overwhelming it. May these pages draw you toward the quiet truth he lived: that God is not far, and a single turn of the heart is enough to find Him.

DEDICATION

To every soul who longs for quiet in a noisy world,
for peace in a restless mind,
and for God in the middle of an ordinary day.

May this book be a doorway,
and may you discover that the One you seek
has already drawn near.

*"But as for me,
the nearness of God is my good."*
-Psalm 73:28

*"My presence shall go with thee,
and I will give thee rest."*
-Exodus 33:14

*"Draw near to God,
and He will draw near to you."*
-James 4:8

Table of Contents

EDITORIAL PREFACE	I
DEDICATION	I
INTRODUCTION	1
What You Will Find in This Book	3
About This Edition	3
A Final Word Before You Begin	4
THE PRACTICE OF THE PRESENCE OF GOD - PREFACE.	5
CONVERSATIONS.	9
LETTERS.	26
A SIMPLE BIOGRAPHY OF BROTHER LAWRENCE	59
LIFE OF BROTHER LAWRENCE	63
A PRACTICAL MANUAL FOR DAILY LIFE HOW TO PRACTICE GOD'S PRESENCE TODAY	65

PRACTICING PRESENCE IN WORK, CREATIVITY, AND
PARENTING   79

PRESENCE WITHOUT PERFECTION   82

A 30-DAY PRACTICE GUIDE   84

CLOSING REFLECTION: A LIFE WITH GOD   86

BROTHER LAWRENCE'S MESSAGE FOR TODAY   96

THE CHRISTIAN HOME AS A PLACE OF DAILY LITURGY   97

WHY THE PSALMS WERE CONSIDERED MEDICINE FOR THE
SOUL   100

WHY SPOKEN BLESSINGS CARRY HEALING POWER   103

A SIMPLE GUIDE TO CARMELITE & MONASTIC MYSTICISM
                                                                106

ANNOTATED GLOSSARY OF SPIRITUAL TERMS   112

Reflective Questions for the Reader's Heart   114

A Closing Meditation   117

Introduction

The Practice of the Presence of God

Brother Lawrence lived in the 1600s, and he was not famous or highly educated. He was a simple man who worked in a kitchen, walked with a limp from an old injury, and described himself as "a great awkward fellow who broke everything." Yet the wisdom he discovered has touched millions of people for more than three hundred years.

What makes Brother Lawrence special is not that he knew a lot about religion, but that he learned how to stay close to God in the middle of everyday life. He believed that God is always near and always ready to meet us—at home, at work, in the kitchen, and even during the busiest and hardest moments of the day. His goal was simple: **to remember God, love God, and speak to God all day long.**

This message feels especially important right now. Our world is fast, loud, and stressful. People are overwhelmed by constant news, responsibilities, screens, and worries. Many feel tired on the inside and unsure how to slow down. Because of this, books about quietness, prayer, and inner peace are becoming popular again.

Brother Lawrence's little book fits perfectly into this moment. It teaches that you do not need special training, long prayers, or a church building to connect with God. You simply turn your heart toward God again and again—during chores, conversations, work, cooking, or moments of rest. For him, **prayer was not something extra you added to life. It was how you lived life.**

He once said, as recorded in the original text:

"The time of business does not with me differ from the time of prayer… I possess God in as great tranquility as if I were upon my knees."

This idea has inspired people who work long hours, parents with busy households, soldiers, teachers, students, caregivers—anyone who wants a sense of peace that does not disappear when life becomes difficult.

What You Will Find in This Book

The book is made of two main parts:

1. **Conversations** people had with Brother Lawrence
2. **Letters** he wrote to friends who wanted help learning to pray

His writing is honest and simple. It does not try to impress or confuse. Instead, it shows how one person learned to stay close to God through love, trust, and constant attention.

By reading slowly and openly, you will begin to see how his simple practice can shape your own life. You may find that peace does not come from running away from the world but from learning to meet God in the middle of it.

About This Edition

After the original text, you will find added notes and guided reflections to help modern readers understand and use Brother Lawrence's insights. These extras include:

- short explanations
- practical steps you can use every day
- reflections that connect his ideas to modern life
- simple exercises for quieting the mind
- background information about Brother Lawrence's life

If you want to read only the original writing, you can stop after the main text.
If you want more help and direction, continue into the commentary and guides after it.

A Final Word Before You Begin

Brother Lawrence believed that God is close, gentle, and involved in every part of our lives. He did not try to escape the world. He learned how to walk with God *inside* the world. He once wrote that spending time with God felt like resting "in the bosom of God" because of the sweetness he experienced.

As you read this book, may you discover a little of that sweetness for yourself—and may this simple way of praying bring peace into the everyday places of your life.

—**Penemue Media**

THE PRACTICE OF THE PRESENCE

OF GOD THE BEST RULE

OF A HOLY LIFE.

BROTHER LAWRENCE.

Being Conversations and Letters of Nicholas Herman, of Lorraine (Brother Lawrence).

PREFACE.

This book consists of notes of several conversations had with, and letters written by Nicholas Herman, of Lorraine, a lowly and unlearned man, who, after having been a footman and soldier, was admitted a Lay Brother among the barefooted Carmelites at Paris in 1666, and was afterwards known as "Brother Lawrence."

His conversion, which took place when he was about eighteen years old, was the result, under God, of the mere sight in midwinter, of a dry and leafless tree, and of the reflections it stirred respecting the change the coming spring would bring. From that time he grew eminently in the knowledge and love of GOD, endeavoring constantly to walk "*as in His presence*." No wilderness wanderings seem to have intervened between the Red Sea and the Jordan of his experience. A wholly consecrated man, he lived his Christian life through as a pilgrim—as a steward and not as an owner, and died at the age of eighty, leaving a name which has been as "ointment poured forth."

The "Conversations" are supposed to have been written by M. Beaufort, Grand Vicar to M. de Chalons, formerly Cardinal de Noailles, by whose recommendation the letters were first published.

The book has, within a short time, gone through repeated English and American editions, and has been a means of blessing to many souls. It contains very much of that wisdom which only lips the Lord has touched can express, and which only hearts He has made teachable can receive.

May this edition also be blessed by GOD, and redound to the praise of the glory of His grace.

CONVERSATIONS.

FIRST CONVERSATION.

The first time I saw *Brother Lawrence*, was upon the 3d of August, 1666. He told me that GOD had done him a singular favor, in his conversion at the age of eighteen.

That in the winter, seeing a tree stripped of its leaves, and considering that within a little time the leaves would be renewed and after that the flowers and fruit appear, he received a high view of the Providence and Power of GOD, which has never since been effaced from his soul. That this view had perfectly set him loose from the world, and kindled in him such a love for GOD, that he could not tell whether it had increased during the more than forty years he had lived since.

That he had been footman to M. Fieubert, the treasurer, and that he was a great awkward fellow who broke everything.

That he had desired to be received into a monastery, thinking that he would there be made to smart for his awkwardness and the faults he should commit, and so he should sacrifice to GOD his life, with its pleasures: but that God had disappointed him, he having met with nothing but satisfaction in that state.

That we should establish ourselves in a sense of GOD'S Presence, by continually conversing with Him. That it was a shameful thing to quit His conversation, to think of trifles and fooleries.

That we should feed and nourish our souls with high notions of GOD; which would yield us great joy in being devoted to Him.

That we ought to *quicken, i.e., to enliven, our faith*. That it was lamentable we had so little; and that instead of taking *faith* for the rule of their conduct, men amused themselves with trivial devotions, which changed daily. That the way of Faith was the spirit of the Church, and that it was sufficient to bring us to a high degree of perfection.

That we ought to give ourselves up to GOD, with regard both to things temporal and spiritual, and seek our satisfaction only in the fulfilling of His will, whether he lead us by suffering or by consolation, for all would lie equal to a soul truly resigned. That there needed fidelity in those dryness, or insensibilities and irksomenesses in prayer, by which GOD tries our love to him; that *then* was the time for us to make good and effectual acts of resignation, whereof one alone would oftentimes very much promote our spiritual advancement.

That as for the miseries and sins he heard of daily in the world, he was so far from wondering at them, that, on the contrary, he was surprised that there were not more, considering the malice sinners were capable of; that for his part he prayed for them; but knowing that GOD could remedy the mischiefs they did when He pleased, he gave himself no farther trouble.

That to arrive at such resignation as GOD requires, we should watch attentively over all the passions which mingle as well in spiritual things as in those of a grosser nature; that GOD would give light concerning those passions to those who truly desire to serve Him. That if this was my design, viz., sincerely to serve GOD, I might come to him (B.

Lawrence) as often as I pleased, without any Fear of being troublesome; but if not, that I ought no more to visit him.

SECOND CONVERSATION.

That he had always been governed by love, without selfish views; and that having resolved to make the love of GOD the *end* of all his actions, he had found reasons to be well satisfied with his method. That he was pleased when he could take up a straw from the ground for the love of GOD, seeking Him only, and nothing else, not even His gifts.

That he had been long troubled in mind from a certain belief that he should be damned; that all the men in the world could not have persuaded him to the contrary; but that he had thus reasoned with himself about it: *I engaged in a religious life only for the love of* GOD, *and I have endeavored to act only for Him; whatever becomes of me, whether I be lost or saved, I will always continue to act purely for the love of* GOD. *I shall have this good at least, that till death I shall have done all that is in me to love Him.* That this trouble of mind had lasted four years; during which time he had suffered much. But that at last he had seen that this trouble arose from want of faith; and that since then he had passed his life in perfect liberty and continual joy. That he had placed his sins betwixt him and GOD, as it were, to tell Him that he did not deserve His favors, but that GOD still continued to bestow them in abundance.

That in order to form a habit of conversing with GOD continually, and referring all we do to Him, we must at first apply to Him with some diligence: but that after a little care we should find His love inwardly excite us to it without any difficulty.

That he expected after the pleasant days GOD had given him, he should have his turn of pain and suffering; but that he was not uneasy about it, knowing very well, that as he could do nothing of himself, GOD would not fail to give him the strength to bear it.

That when an occasion of practicing some virtue offered, he addressed himself to GOD, saying, LORD, *I cannot do this unless Thou enablest me*: and that then he received strength more than sufficient.

That when he had failed in his duty, he only confessed his fault, saying to GOD, *I shall never do otherwise, if You leave me to myself; it is You who must hinder my falling, and mend what is amiss*. That after this, he gave himself no further uneasiness about it.

That we ought to act with GOD in the greatest simplicity, speaking to Him frankly and plainly, and imploring His assistance in our affairs, just as they happen. That GOD never failed to grant it, as he had often experienced.

That he had been lately sent into Burgundy, to buy the provision of wine for the society, which was a very unwelcome task for him, because he had no turn for business, and because he was lame and could not go about the boat but by rolling himself over the casks. That however he gave himself no uneasiness about it, nor about the purchase of the wine. That he said to GOD, *It was His business he was about*, and that he afterwards found it very well performed. That he had been sent into Auvergne, the year before, upon the same account; that he could not tell how the matter passed, but that it proved very well.

So, likewise, in his business in the kitchen (to which he had naturally a great aversion), having accustomed himself to do everything there for the love of GOD, and with prayer, upon all occasions, for His grace to do his work well, he had found everything easy, during fifteen years that he had been employed there.

That he was very well pleased with the post he was now in; but that he was as ready to quit that as the former, since he was always pleasing himself in every condition, by doing little things for the love of GOD.

That with him the set times of prayer were not different from other times; that he retired to pray, according to the directions of his Superior, but that he did not want such retirement, nor ask for it, because his greatest business did not divert him from GOD.

That as he knew his obligation to love GOD in all things, and as he endeavored so to do, he had no need of a director to advise him, but that he needed much a Confessor to absolve him. That he was very sensible of his faults, but not discouraged by them; that he confessed them to GOD, but did not plead against Him to excuse them. When he had so done, he peaceably resumed his usual practice of love and adoration.

That in his trouble of mind, he had consulted nobody, but knowing only by the light of faith that GOD was present, he contented himself with directing all his actions to Him, *i.e.*, doing them with a desire to please Him, let what would come of it.

That useless thoughts spoil all: that the mischief began there; but that we ought to reject them, as soon as we perceived their impertinence to the matter in hand, or our salvation; and return to our communion with GOD.

That at the beginning he had often passed his time appointed for prayer, in rejecting wandering thoughts, and falling back into them. That he could never regulate his devotion by certain methods as some do. That nevertheless, at first he had *meditated* for some time, but afterwards that went off, in a manner he could give no account of.

That all bodily mortifications and other exercises are useless, except as they serve to arrive at the union with GOD by love; that he had well considered this, and found it the shortest way to go straight to Him by a continual exercise of love, and doing all things for His sake.

That we ought to make a great difference between the acts of the *understanding* and those of the *will*: that the first were comparatively of little value, and the others, all. That our only business was to love and delight ourselves in GOD.

That all possible kinds of mortification, if they were void of the love of GOD, could not efface a single sin. That we ought, without anxiety, to expect the pardon of our sins from the Blood of JESUS CHRIST, only endeavoring to love Him with all our hearts. That GOD seemed to have granted the greatest favors to the greatest sinners, as more signal monuments of his mercy.

That the greatest pains or pleasures of this world, were not to be compared with what he had experienced of both kinds in a spiritual state: so that he was careful for nothing and feared nothing, desiring only one thing of GOD, viz., that he might not offend Him.

That he had no scruples; for, said he, when I *fail* in my duty, I readily acknowledge it, saying, *I am used to do so: I shall never do otherwise, if I am left to myself*. I fail not, then I give GOD thanks, acknowledging the strength comes from Him.

THIRD CONVERSATION.

He told me that the *foundation of the spiritual life* in *him*, had been a high notion and esteem of GOD in faith; which when he had once well conceived, he had no other care at first, but faithfully to reject every other thought, *that he might perform all his actions for the love of* GOD. That when sometimes he had not thought of GOD for a good while, he did not disquiet himself for it; but after having acknowledged his wretchedness to GOD, he returned to Him with so much the greater trust in Him, as he had found himself wretched through forgetting Him.

That the trust we put in GOD, honors Him much, and draws down great graces.

That it was impossible, not only that GOD should deceive, hut also that He should long let a soul suffer which is perfectly resigned to Him, and resolved to endure everything for His sake.

That he had so often experienced the ready succors of Divine Grace upon all occasions, that from the same experience, when he had business to do, he did not think of it beforehand; but when it was time to do it, he found in GOD, as in a clear mirror, all that was fit for him to do. That of late he had acted thus, without anticipating care; but before the experience above mentioned, he had used it in his affairs.

When outward business diverted him a little from the thought of GOD, a fresh remembrance coming from GOD invested his soul, and so inflamed and transported him that it was difficult for him to contain himself.

That he was more united to GOD in his outward employments, than when he left them for devotion in retirement.

That he expected hereafter some great pain of body or mind; that the worst that could happen to him was, to lose that sense of GOD which he had enjoyed so long; but that the goodness of GOD assured him He would not forsake him utterly, and that He would give him strength to bear whatever evil He permitted to happen to him; and therefore that he feared nothing, and had no occasion to consult with anybody about his state. That when he had attempted to do it, he had always come away more perplexed; and that as he was conscious of his readiness to lay down his life for the love of GOD, he had no apprehension of danger. That perfect resignation to GOD was a sure way to heaven, a way in which we had always sufficient light for our conduct.

That in the beginning of the spiritual life, we ought to be faithful in doing our duty and denying ourselves; but after that, unspeakable pleasures followed; that in difficulties we need only have recourse to JESUS CHRIST, and beg his grace; with that everything became easy.

That many do not advance in the Christian progress because they stick in penances, and particular exercises, while they neglect the love of GOD, which is the *end*. That this appeared plainly by their works, and was the *reason* why we see so little solid virtue.

That there needed neither art nor science for going to GOD, but only a heart resolutely determined to apply itself to nothing but Him, or for *His* sake, and to love him only.

FOURTH CONVERSATION.

He discoursed with me very frequently, and with great openness of heart concerning his manner of *going* to GOD, whereof some part is related already.

He told me that all consists *in one hearty renunciation* of everything which we are sensible does not lead to GOD; that we might accustom ourselves to a continual conversation with Him, with freedom and in simplicity. That we need only to recognize GOD intimately present with us, to address ourselves to Him every moment, that we may beg His assistance for knowing His will in things doubtful, and for rightly performing those which we plainly see he requires of us, offering them to Him before we do them, and giving Him thanks when we have done.

That in this conversation with God, we are also employed in praising, adoring and loving Him incessantly, for His infinite goodness and perfection.

That, without being discouraged on account of our sins, we should pray for His grace with a perfect confidence, as relying upon the infinite merits of our LORD JESUS CHRIST. That GOD never failed offering us His grace at each action; that he distinctly perceived it, and never failed of it, unless when his thoughts had wandered from a sense of GOD'S Presence, or he had forgotten to ask His assistance.

That GOD always gave us light in our doubts, when we had no other design but ask to please Him.

That our sanctification did not depend upon *changing* our works, but in doing that for GOD's sake, which we commonly do for our own. That it was lamentable to see how many people mistook the means for the end, addicting themselves to certain works, which they performed very imperfectly, by reason of their human or selfish regards.

That the most excellent method he had found of going to GOD, was that of doing our common business without any view of pleasing men,[1] and (as far as we are capable) purely for the love of GOD.

That it was a great delusion to think that the times of prayer ought to differ from other times: that we are as strictly obliged to adhere to GOD by action in the time of action, as by prayer in the season of prayer.

That his prayer was nothing else but a sense of the presence of GOD, his soul being at that time insensible to everything but Divine love: and that when the appointed times of prayer were past, he found no difference, because he still continued with GOD, praising and blessing Him with all his might, so that he passed his life in continual joy; yet hoped that GOD would give him somewhat to suffer, when he should grow stronger.

That we ought, once for all, heartily to put our whole trust in GOD, and make a total surrender of ourselves to Him, secure that He would not deceive us.

That we ought not to be weary of doing little things for the love of GOD, who regards not the greatness of the work, but the love with

---

[1] Gal. i, 10; Eph. vi, 5, 6.

which it is performed. That we should not wonder if, in the beginning, we often failed in our endeavors, but that at last we should gain a habit, which will naturally produce its acts in us, without our care, and to our exceeding great delight.

That the whole substance of religion was faith, hope and charity; by the practice of which we become united to the will of GOD: that all besides is indifferent, and to be used as a means that we may arrive at our end, and be swallowed up therein, by faith and charity.

That all things are possible to him who *believes*—that they are less difficult to him who *hopes*—that they are more easy to him who *loves*, and still more easy to him who perseveres in the practice of these three virtues.

That the end we ought to propose to ourselves is to become, in this life, the most perfect worshippers of GOD we can possibly be, as we hope to be through all eternity.

That when we enter upon the spiritual life, we should consider, and examine to the bottom, what we are. And then we should find ourselves worthy of all contempt, and not deserving indeed the name of Christians: subject to all kinds of misery and numberless accidents, which trouble us and cause perpetual vicissitudes in our health, in our humors, in our internal and external dispositions; in fine, persons whom GOD would humble by many pains and labors, as well within as without. After this we should not wonder that troubles, temptations, oppositions and contradictions happen to us from men. We ought, on the contrary, to submit ourselves to them, and bear them as long as GOD pleases, as things highly advantageous to us.

That the greater perfection a soul aspires after, the more dependent it is upon Divine grace.

[2] Being questioned by one of his own society (to whom he was obliged to open himself) by what means he had attained such an habitual sense of GOD, he told him that, since his first coming to the monastery, he had considered GOD as the end of all his thoughts and desires, as the mark to which they should tend, and in which they should terminate.

That in the beginning of his novitiate, he spent the hours appointed for private prayer in thinking of GOD, so as to convince his mind of, and to impress deeply upon his heart, the Divine existence, rather by devout sentiments, and submission to the lights of faith, than by studied reasonings and elaborate meditations. That by this short and sure method, he exercised himself in the knowledge and love of GOD, resolving to use his utmost endeavor to live, in a continual sense of His Presence, and if possible, never to forget Him more.

That when he had thus in prayer filled his mind with great sentiments of that infinite Being, he went to his work appointed in the kitchen (for he was cook to the society); there having first considered severally the things his office required, and when and how each thing was to be done, he spent all the intervals of his time, as well before as after his work, in prayer.

That when he began his business, he said to GOD, with a filial trust in Him, "O my GOD, since Thou art with me, and I must now, in

---

[2] The particulars which follow are collected from other accounts of Brother Lawrence

obedience to Thy commands, apply my mind to these outward things, I beseech Thee to grant me the grace to continue in Thy Presence; and to this end do Thou prosper me with Thy assistance, receive all my works, and possess all my affections."

As he proceeded in his work, he continued his familiar conversation with his Maker,—imploring His grace, and offering to Him all his actions.

When he had finished, he examined himself how he had discharged his duty; if he found *well*, he returned thanks to GOD; if otherwise, he asked pardon; and without being discouraged, he set his mind right again, and continued his exercise of the *presence* of GOD, as if he had never deviated from it. "Thus," said he, "by rising after my falls, and by frequently renewed acts of faith and love, I am come to a state wherein it would be as difficult for me not to think of GOD as it was at first to accustom myself to it."

As brother Lawrence had found such an advantage in walking in the presence of GOD, it was natural for him to recommend it earnestly to others; but his example was a stronger inducement than any arguments he could propose. His very countenance was edifying, such a sweet and calm devotion appearing in it as could not but effect the beholders. And it was observed that in the greatest hurry of business in the kitchen, he still preserved his recollection and heavenly-mindedness. He was never hasty nor loitering, but did each thing in its season, with an even, uninterrupted composure and tranquility of spirit. "The time of business," said he, "does not with me differ from the time of prayer; and in the noise and clatter of my kitchen, while several persons are at the same time calling for different things, I possess GOD in as great tranquility as if I were upon my knees at the blessed sacrament."

LETTERS.

FIRST LETTER.

Since you desire so earnestly that I should communicate to you the method by which I arrived at that *habitual sense of* GOD'S *Presence*, which our LORD, of His mercy, has been pleased to vouch-safe to me, I must tell you that it is with great difficulty that I am prevailed on by your importunities; and now I do it only upon the terms that you show my letter to nobody. If I knew that you should let it be seen, all the desire that I have for your advancement would not be able to determine me to it. The account I can give you is:

Having found in many books different methods of going to GOD, and divers practices of the spiritual life, I thought this would serve rather to puzzle me than facilitate what I sought after, which was nothing but how to become wholly GOD'S. This made me resolve to give the all for the all; so after having given myself wholly to GOD, that He might take away my sin, *I renounced, for the love of Him, everything that was not He; and I began to live as if there was none but He and I in the world.* Sometimes I considered myself before Him as a poor criminal at the feet of his judge; at other times I beheld Him in my heart as my FATHER, as my GOD: I worshipped Him the oftenest that I could, keeping my mind in His holy Presence, and recalling it as often as I found it wandered from Him. I found no small pain in this exercise, and yet I continued it, notwithstanding all the difficulties that occurred, without troubling or disquieting myself when my mind had wandered involuntarily. I made this my business as much all the day long as at the appointed times of prayer; for at all times, every hour, every minute, even in the height of my business, I drove away from my mind everything that was capable of interrupting my thought of GOD.

Such has been my common practice ever since I entered in religion; and, though I have done it very imperfectly, yet I have found great advantages by it. These, I well know, are to be imputed to the mere mercy and goodness of GOD, because we can do nothing without Him; and *I* still less than any. But when we are faithful to keep ourselves in His holy Presence, and set Him always before us, this not only hinders our offending Him, and doing anything that may displease Him, at least wilfully, but it also begets in us a holy freedom, and, if I may so speak, a familiarity with GOD, wherewith we ask, and that successfully, the graces we stand in need of. In fine, by often repeating these acts, they become *habitual*, and the presence of GOD rendered as it were *natural to* us Give Him thanks, if you please, with me, for His great goodness towards me, which I can never sufficiently admire, for the many favors He has done to so miserable a sinner as I am. May all things praise Him. Amen.

I am, in our LORD, yours, &c.

SECOND LETTER.

To the Reverend—

Not finding my manner of life in books, although I have no difficulty about it, yet, for greater security, I shall be glad to know your thoughts concerning it.

In a conversation some days since with a person of piety, he told me the spiritual life was a life of grace, which begins with servile fear, which is increased by hope of eternal life, and which is consummated by pure love. That each of these states had its different stages, by which one arrives at last at that blessed consummation.

I have not followed all these methods. On the contrary, from I know not what instincts, I found they discouraged me. This was the reason why, at my entrance into religion, I took a resolution to give myself up to GOD, as the best return I could make for His love; and, for the love of Him, to renounce all besides.

For the first year I commonly employed myself during the time set apart for devotion with the thought of death, judgment, heaven, hell, and my sins, Thus continued some years, applying my mind carefully the rest of the day, and even in the midst of my business, *to the presence of* GOD, whom I considered always as *with* me, often as *in* me.

At length I came insensibly to do the same thing during my set time of prayer, which caused in me great delight and consolation. This practice produced in me so high an esteem for GOD, that *faith* alone was capable to satisfy me in that point.[3]

Such was my beginning; and yet I must tell you that for the first ten years I suffered much: the apprehension that I was not devoted to GOD as I wished to be, my past sins always present to my mind, and the great unmerited favors which GOD did me, were the matter and source of my sufferings. During this time I fell often, and rose again presently. It seemed to me that all creatures, reason, and GOD Himself were against me; and *faith* alone for me. I was troubled sometimes with thoughts that to believe I had received such favors was an effect of my presumption, which pretended to be *at once* where others arrive with difficulty; at other times that it was a wilful delusion, and that there was no salvation for me.

When I thought of nothing but to end my days in these troubles (which did not at all diminish the trust I had in GOD, and which served only to increase my faith), I found myself changed all at once; and my soul, which, till that time, was in trouble, felt a profound inward peace, as if she were in her centre and place of rest.

Ever since that time I walk before GOD simply, in faith, with humility and with love; and I apply myself diligently to do nothing and think nothing which may displease Him. I hope that when I have done what I can, He will do with me what He pleases.

---

[3] *I suppose he means* that all distinct notions he could form of GOD, were unsatisfactory, because he perceived them to be unworthy of GOD; and therefore his mind was not to be satisfied but by the views of *faith*, which apprehend GOD as infinite and incomprehensible, as He is in Himself, and not as He can be conceived by human ideas.

As for what passes in me at present, I cannot express it. I have no pain or difficulty about my state, because I have no will but that of GOD, which I endeavor to accomplish in all things, and to which I am so resigned that I would not take up a straw from the ground against His order, or from any other motive than purely that of love to Him.

I have quitted all forms of devotion and set prayers but those to which my state obliges me. And I make it my business only to persevere in His holy presence, wherein I keep myself by a simple attention, and a general fond regard to GOD, which I may call an *actual presence of* GOD; or, to speak better, an habitual, silent and secret conversation of the soul with GOD, which often causes me joys and raptures inwardly, and sometimes also outwardly, so great, that I am forced to use means to moderate them and prevent their appearance to others.

In short, I am assured beyond all doubt that my soul has been with GOD above these thirty years. I pass over many things that I may not be tedious to you, yet I think it proper to inform you after what manner I consider myself before GOD, whom I behold as my King.

I consider myself as the most wretched of men, full of sores and corruption, and who has committed all sorts of crimes against his King; touched with a sensible regret, I confess to him all my wickedness, I ask His forgiveness, I abandon myself in His hands that He may do what he pleases with me. The King, full of mercy and goodness, very far from chastising me, embraces me with love, makes me eat at His table, serves me with His own hands, gives me the key of His treasures; He converses and delights Himself with me incessantly, in a thousand and a thousand ways, and treats me in all respects as His favorite. It is thus I consider myself from time to time in His holy presence.

My most useful method is this simple attention, and such a general passionate regard to GOD; to whom I find myself often attached with greater sweetness and delight than that of an infant at the mother's breast; so that, if I dare use the expression, I should choose to call this state the bosom, of GOD, for the inexpressible sweetness which I taste and experience there.

If sometimes my thoughts wander from it by necessity or infirmity, I am presently recalled by inward motions so charming and delicious that I am ashamed to mention them. I desire your reverence to reflect rather upon my great wretchedness, of which you are fully informed, than upon the great favors which GOD does me, all unworthy and ungrateful as I am.

As for my set hours of prayer, they are only a continuation of the same exercise. Sometimes I consider myself there as a stone before a carver, whereof he is to make a statue; presenting myself thus before GOD, I desire Him to form His perfect image in my soul, and make me entirely like Himself.

At other times, when I apply myself to prayer, I feel all my spirit and all my soul lift itself up without any care or effort of mine, and it continues as it were suspended and firmly fixed in GOD, as in its centre and place of rest.

I know that some charge this state with inactivity, delusion and self-love. I confess that it is a holy inactivity, and would be a happy self-love, if the soul in that state were capable of it; because, in effect, while she is in this repose, she cannot be disturbed by such acts as she was formerly accustomed to, and which were then her support, but which would now rather hinder than assist her.

Yet I cannot bear that this should be called delusion; because the soul which thus enjoys GOD desires herein nothing but Him. If this be delusion in me, it belongs to GOD to remedy it. Let Him do what He pleases with me; I desire only Him, and to be wholly devoted to Him. You will, however, oblige me in sending me your opinion, to which I always pay a great deference, for I have a singular esteem for your reverence, and am in our LORD,

Yours, &c.

THIRD LETTER.

We have a GOD who is infinitely gracious and knows all our wants. I always thought that He would reduce you to extremity. He will come in His own time, and when you least expect it. Hope in Him more than ever; thank Him with me for the favors he does you, particularly for the fortitude and patience which He gives you in your afflictions. It is a plain mark of the care He takes of you. Comfort yourself, then, with Him, and give thanks for all.

I admire also the fortitude and bravery of Mr. ——. God has given him a good disposition and a good will; but there is in him still a little of the world, and a great deal of youth. I hope the affliction which GOD has sent him will prove a wholesome remedy to him, and make him enter into himself. It is an accident which should engage him to put all his trust in *Him* who accompanies him everywhere. Let him think of Him as often as he can, especially in the greatest dangers. A little lifting up of the heart suffices. A little remembrance of GOD, one act of inward worship, though upon a march, and a sword in hand, are prayers, which, however short, are nevertheless very acceptable to GOD; and far from lessening a soldier's courage in occasions of danger, they best serve to fortify it.

Let him then think of GOD the most he can. Let him accustom himself, by degrees, to this small but holy exercise. No one will notice it, and nothing is easier than to repeat often in the day these little internal adorations. Recommend to him, if you please, that he think of GOD the most he can, in the manner here directed. It is very fit and most necessary for a soldier, who is daily exposed to the dangers of life. I hope that GOD will assist him and all the family, to whom I present my service, being theirs and Yours, &c.

FOURTH LETTER.

I have taken this opportunity to communicate to you the sentiments of one of our society, concerning the admirable effects and continual assistances which he receives from *the presence of* GOD. Let you and me both profit by them.

You must know his continual care has been, for about forty years past that he has spent in religion, to be *always with* GOD, and to do nothing, say nothing, and think nothing which may displease Him; and this without any other view than purely for the love of Him, and because he deserves infinitely more.

He is now so accustomed to that *Divine Presence*, that he receives from it continual succors upon all occasions. For about thirty years, his soul has been filled with joys so continual, and sometimes so great, that he is forced to use means to moderate them, and to hinder their appearing outwardly.

If sometimes he is a little too much absent from that *Divine Presence*, GOD presently makes Himself to be felt in his soul to recall him, which often happens when he is most engaged in his outward business. He answers with exact fidelity to these inward drawings, either by an elevation of his heart towards GOD, or by a meek and fond regard to Him, or by such words as love forms upon these occasions, as for instance, *My God, here I am all devoted to Thee*: LORD, *make me according to Thy heart.* And then it seems to him (as in effect he feels it) that this GOD of love, satisfied with such few words, reposes again, and rests in the fund and centre of his soul. The experience of these things gives him such an assurance that GOD is always in the fund or bottom of his soul, that it renders him incapable of doubting it upon any account whatever.

Judge by this what content and satisfaction he enjoys while he continually finds in himself so great a treasure. He is no longer in an anxious search after it, but has it open before him, and may take what he pleases of it.

He complains much of our blindness, and cries often that we are to be pitied who content ourselves with so little. GOD, saith he, *has infinite treasure to bestow, and we take up with a little sensible devotion, which passes in a moment. Blind as we are, we hinder GOD, and stop the current of His graces. But when He finds a soul penetrated with a lively faith, He pours into it His graces and favors plentifully: there they flow like a torrent, which, after being forcibly stopped against its ordinary course, when it has found a passage, spreads itself with impetuosity and abundance.*

Yes, we often stop this torrent by the little value we set upon it. But let us stop it no more; let us enter into ourselves and break down the bank which hinders it. Let us make way for grace; let us redeem the lost time, for perhaps we have but little left. Death follows us close; let us be well prepared for it: for we die but once; and a miscarriage *there* is irretrievable.

I say again, let us enter into ourselves. The time presses, there is no room for delay: our souls are at stake. I believe you have taken such effectual measures that you will not be surprised. I commend you for it; it is the one thing necessary. We must, nevertheless, always work at it, because not to advance in the spiritual life is to go back. But those who have the gale of the HOLY SPIRIT go forward even in sleep. If the vessel of our soul is still tossed with winds and storms, let us awake the LORD, who reposes in it, and He will quickly calm the sea.

    I have taken the liberty to impart to you these good sentiments, that you may compare them with your own. It will serve again to kindle and inflame them, if by misfortune (which GOD forbid, for it would be indeed a great misfortune) they should be, though never so little, cooled. Let us then *both* recall our first fervors. Let us profit by the example and the sentiments of this brother, who is little known of the world, but known of GOD, and extremely caressed by Him. I will pray for you; do you pray instantly for me, who am, in our LORD.

Yours, &c.

FIFTH LETTER.

I received this day two books and a letter from Sister ——, who is preparing to make her profession, and upon that account desires the prayers of your holy society, and yours in particular. I perceive that she reckons much upon them; pray do not disappoint her. Beg of GOD that she may make her sacrifice in the view of His love alone, and with a firm resolution to be wholly devoted to Him. I will send you one of these books which treat of *the presence of* GOD; a subject which, in my opinion, contains the whole spiritual life; and it seems to me that whoever duly practices it will soon become spiritual.

I know that for the right practice of it, the heart must be empty of all other things; because GOD will possess the heart *alone*; and as He cannot possess it *alone* without emptying it of all besides, so neither can He act *there*, and do in it what He pleases, unless it be left vacant to Him.

There is not in the world a kind of life more sweet and delightful than that of a continual conversation with GOD. Those only can comprehend it who practice and experience it; yet I do not advise you to do it from that motive. It is not pleasure which we ought to seek in this exercise; but let us do it from a principle of love, and because GOD would have us.

Were I a preacher, I should, above all other things, preach the practice of *the presence of* GOD; and, were I a director, I should advise all the world to do it, so necessary do I think it, and so easy too.

Ah! knew we but the want we have of the grace and assistance of GOD, we should never lose sight of Him, no, not for a moment. Believe me; make immediately a holy and firm resolution never more wilfully to forget Him, and to spend the rest of your days in His sacred presence, deprived for the love of Him, if He thinks fit, of all consolations.

Set heartily about this work, and if you do it as you ought, be assured that you will soon find the effects of it. I will assist you with my prayers, poor as they are. I recommend myself earnestly to yours and those of your holy society being theirs, and more particularly

Yours, &c.

SIXTH LETTER.

To the Same.

I have received from Mrs. ——, the things which you gave her for me. I wonder that you have not given me your thoughts of the little book I sent to you, and which you must have received. Pray set heartily about the practice of it in your old age: it is better late than never.

I cannot imagine how religious persons can live satisfied without the practice of *the presence of* GOD. For my part. I keep myself retired with Him in the fund or centre of my soul as much as I can; and while I am so with Him I fear nothing, but the least turning from Him is insupportable.

This exercise does not much fatigue the body; it is, however, proper to deprive it sometimes, nay often; of many little pleasures which are innocent and lawful, for GOD will not permit that a soul which desires to be devoted entirely to Him should take other pleasures than with Him: that is more than reasonable.

I do not say that therefore we must put any violent constraint upon ourselves. No, we must serve GOD in a holy freedom; we must do our business faithfully; without trouble or disquiet, recalling our mind to GOD mildly, and with tranquility, as often as we find it wandering from Him.

It is, however, necessary to put our whole trust in GOD, laying aside all other cares, and even some particular forms of devotion, though very good in themselves, yet such as one often engages in unreasonably, because these devotions are only means to attain to the end. So when by this exercise of *the presence of* GOD we are *with Him* who is our end, it is then useless to return to the means; but we may continue with Him our commerce of love, persevering in His holy presence, one while by an act of praise, of adoration or of desire; one while by an act of resignation or thanksgiving; and in all the ways which our spirit can invent.

Be not discouraged by the repugnance which you may find in it from nature; you must do yourself violence. At the first one often thinks it lost time, but you must go on, and resolve to persevere in it to death, notwithstanding all the difficulties that may occur. I recommend myself to the prayers of your holy society, and yours in particular. I am, in our LORD,

Yours, &c.

SEVENTH LETTER.

I pity you much. It will be of great importance if you can leave the care of your affairs to ——, and spend the remainder of your life only in worshiping GOD. He requires no great matters of us; a little remembrance of Him from time to time; a little adoration; sometimes to pray for His grace, sometimes to offer Him your sufferings, and sometimes to return Him thanks for the favors He has given you, and still gives you, in the midst of your troubles, and to console yourself with Him the oftenest you can. Lift up your heart to Him, sometimes even at your meals, and when you are in company: the least little remembrance will always be acceptable to Him. You need not cry very loud; He is nearer to us than we are aware of.

It is not necessary for being with GOD to be always at church: we may make an oratory of our heart wherein to retire from time to time to converse with Him in meekness, humility and love. Every one is capable of such familiar conversation with GOD, some more, some less: He knows what we can do. Let us begin, then. Perhaps He expects but one generous resolution on our part. Have courage. We have but little time to live; you are near sixty-four, and I am almost eighty. Let us live and die with GOD. Sufferings will be sweet and pleasant to us while we are with Him; and the greatest pleasures will be, without Him, a cruel punishment to us. May He be blessed for all. Amen.

Accustom yourself, then, by degrees thus to worship Him, to beg His grace, to offer Him your heart from time to time in the midst of your business, even every moment, if you can. Do not always scrupulously confine yourself to certain rules, or particular forms of devotion, but act with a general confidence in GOD, with love and humility. You may assure —— of my poor prayers, and that I am their servant, and particularly

Yours in our LORD, &c.

EIGHTH LETTER.

(Concerning wandering thoughts in Prayer.)

You tell me nothing new; you are not the only one that is troubled with wandering thoughts. Our mind is extremely roving; but, as the will is mistress of all our faculties, she must recall them, and carry them to GOD as their last end.

When the mind, for want of being sufficiently reduced by recollection at our first engaging in devotion, has contracted certain bad habits of wandering and dissipation, they are difficult to overcome, and commonly draw us, even against our wills, to the things of the earth.

I believe one remedy for this is to confess our faults, and to humble ourselves before GOD. I do not advise you to use multiplicity of words in prayer: many words and long discourses being often the occasions of wandering. Hold yourself in prayer before GOD, like a dumb or paralytic beggar at a rich man's gate. Let it be *your* business to keep your mind in the presence of the LORD. If it sometimes wander and withdraw itself from Him, do not much disquiet yourself for that: trouble and disquiet serve rather to distract the mind than to re-collect it: the will must bring it back in tranquility. If you persevere in this manner, GOD will have pity on you.

One way to re-collect the mind easily in the time of prayer, and preserve it more in tranquility, is *not to let it wander too far at other times*: you should keep it strictly in the presence of GOD; and being accustomed to think of Him often, you will find it easy to keep your mind calm in the time of prayer, or at least to recall it from its wanderings.

I have told you already at large, in my former letters, of the advantages we may draw from this practice of the presence of GOD: let us set about it seriously, and pray for one another.

Yours, &c.

NINTH LETTER.

The enclosed is an answer to that which I received from ——; pray deliver it to her. She seems to me full of good will, but she would go faster than grace. One does not become holy all at once. I recommend her to you: we ought to help one another by our advice, and yet more by our good examples. You will oblige me to let me hear of her from time to time, and whether she be very fervent and very obedient.

Let us thus think often that our only business in this life is to please GOD, and that all besides is but folly and vanity. You and I have lived about forty years in religion (*i.e.*, a monastic life). Have we employed them in loving and serving GOD, who by His mercy has called us to this state and for that very end? I am filled with shame and confusion when I reflect on one hand upon the great favors which GOD has done, and incessantly continues to do me; and on the other, upon the ill use I have made of them, and my small advancement in the way of perfection.

Since by His mercy He gives us still a little time, let us begin in earnest: let us repair the lost time: let us return with a full assurance to that FATHER of mercies, who is always ready to receive us affectionately. Let us renounce, let us generously renounce, for the love of Him, all that is not Himself; He deserves infinitely more. Let us think of Him perpetually. Let us put all our trust in Him. I doubt not but we shall soon find the effects of it in receiving the abundance of His grace, with which we can do all things, and without which we can do nothing but sin.

We cannot escape the dangers which abound in life without the actual and *continual* help of GOD: let us then pray to Him for it *continually*. How can we pray to Him without being with Him? How can we be with Him but in thinking of Him often? And how can we often think of Him, but by a holy habit which we should form of it? You will tell me that I am always saying the same thing. It is true, for this is the best and easiest method I know; and as I use no other, I advise all the world to do it. We must *know* before we can *love*. In order to *know* GOD, we must often *think* of Him; and when we come to *love* Him, we shall then also think of Him often, for our heart will be with our treasure. This is an argument which well deserves your consideration.

I am, Yours, &c.

TENTH LETTER.

I have had a good deal of difficulty to bring myself to write to Mr. ——, and I do it now purely because you and Madam —— desire me. Pray write the directions and send it to him. I am very well pleased with the trust which you have in GOD: I wish that He may increase it in you more and more. We cannot have too much in so good and faithful a Friend, who will never fail us in this world nor in the next.

If Mr. —— makes his advantage of the loss he has had, and puts all his confidence in GOD, He will soon give him another friend, more powerful and more inclined to serve him. He disposes of hearts as He pleases. Perhaps Mr. —— was too much attached to him he has lost. We ought to love our friends, but without encroaching upon the love due to GOD, which must be the principal.

Pray remember what I have recommended to you, which is, to think often on GOD, by day, by night, in your business, and even in your diversions. He is always near you and with you: leave Him not alone. You would think it rude to leave a friend alone who came to visit you: why then must GOD be neglected? Do not then forget Him, but think on Him often, adore Him continually, live and die with Him; this is the glorious employment of a Christian. In a word, this is our profession; if we do not know it, we must learn it. I will endeavor to help you with my prayers, and am, in our LORD, Yours, &c.

ELEVENTH LETTER.

I do not pray that you may be delivered from your pains, but I pray GOD earnestly that He would give you strength and patience to bear them as long as He pleases. Comfort yourself with Him who holds you fastened to the cross. He will loose you when He thinks fit. Happy those who suffer with Him: accustom yourself to suffer in that manner, and seek from Him the strength to endure as much, and as long, as He shall judge to be necessary for you. The men of the world do not comprehend these truths, nor is it to be wondered at, since they suffer like what they are, and not like Christians. They consider sickness as a pain to nature, and not as a favor from GOD; and seeing it only in that light, they find nothing in it but grief and distress. But those who consider sickness as coming from the hand of GOD, as the effect of His mercy, and the means which He employs for their salvation—such, commonly find in it great sweetness and sensible consolation.

I wish you could convince yourself that GOD is often (in some sense) nearer to us, and more effectually present with us, in sickness than in health. Rely upon no other Physician; for, according to my apprehension, He reserves your cure to Himself. Put, then, all your trust in Him, and you will soon find the effects of it in your recovery, which we often retard by putting greater confidence in physic than in GOD.

Whatever remedies you make use of, they will succeed only so far as He permits. When pains come from GOD, He only can cure them. He often sends diseases of the body to cure those of the soul. Comfort yourself with the sovereign Physician both of the soul and body.

Be satisfied with the condition in which GOD places you: however happy you may think me, I envy you. Pains and sufferings would be a paradise to me while I should suffer with my GOD; and the greatest pleasures would be hell to me if I could relish them without Him. All my consolation would be to suffer something for His sake.

I must, in a little time, go to GOD. What comforts me in this life is, that I now see Him *by faith*; and I see Him in such a manner as might make me say sometimes, *I believe no more, but I see*. I feel what faith teaches us, and in that assurance and that practice of faith, I will live and die with Him.

Continue then always with GOD: it is the only support and comfort for your affliction. I shall beseech Him to be with you. I present my service.

Yours, &c.

TWELFTH LETTER.

If we were well accustomed to the exercise of *the presence of* GOD, all bodily diseases would be much alleviated thereby. GOD often permits that we should suffer a little to purify our souls and oblige us to continue *with* Him.

Take courage: offer Him your pains incessantly: pray to Him for strength to endure them. Above all, get a habit of entertaining yourself often with GOD, and forget Him the least you can. Adore Him in your infirmities, offer yourself to Him from time to time, and in the height of your sufferings, beseech Him humbly and affectionately (as a child his father) to make you conformable to His holy-will. I shall endeavor to assist you with my poor prayers.

GOD has many ways of drawing us to Himself. He sometimes hides Himself from us, but *faith* alone, which will not fail us in time of need, ought to be our support, and the foundation of our confidence, which must be all in GOD.

I know not how GOD will dispose of me. I am always happy. All the world suffer; and I, who deserve the severest discipline, feel joys so continual and so great that I can scarce contain them.

I would willingly ask of GOD a part of your sufferings, but that I know my weakness, which is so great, that if He left me one moment to myself I should be the most wretched man alive. And yet I know not how He can leave me alone, because faith gives me as strong a conviction as sense can do, that He never forsakes us until we have first forsaken Him. Let us fear to leave Him. Let us be always with Him. Let us live and die in His presence. Do you pray for me, as I for you.

I am, Yours, &c.

THIRTEENTH LETTER.

To the Same.

I am in pain to see you suffer so long. What gives me some ease and sweetens the feelings I have for your griefs is, that they are proofs of GOD'S love towards you. See them in that view and you will bear them more easily. As your case is, it is my opinion that you should leave off human remedies, and resign yourself entirely to the providence of GOD: perhaps He stays only for that resignation and a perfect trust in Him to cure you. Since, notwithstanding all your cares, physic has hitherto proved unsuccessful, and your malady still increases, it will not be tempting GOD to abandon yourself in His hands, and expect all from Him.

I told you in my last that He sometimes permits bodily diseases to cure the distempers of the soul. Have courage then: make a virtue of necessity. Ask of GOD, not deliverance from your pains, but strength to bear resolutely, for the love of Him, all that He should please, and as long as He shall please.

Such prayers, indeed, are a little hard to nature, but most acceptable to GOD, and sweet to those that love Him. Love sweetens pains; and when one loves GOD, one suffers for His sake with joy and courage. Do you so, I beseech you: comfort yourself with Him, who is the only Physician of all our maladies. He is the FATHER of the afflicted, always ready to help us. He loves us infinitely more than we imagine. Love Him, then, and seek no consolation elsewhere. I hope you will soon receive it. Adieu. I will help you with my prayers, poor as they are, and shall always be, in our LORD Yours, &c.

FOURTEENTH LETTER.

To the Same.

I render thanks to our LORD for having relieved you a little, according to your desire. I have been often near expiring, but I never was so much satisfied as then. Accordingly, I did not pray for any relief, but I prayed for strength to suffer with courage, humility and love. Ah, how sweet it is to suffer with GOD! However great the sufferings may be, receive them with love. It is paradise to suffer and be with Him; so that if in this life we would enjoy the peace of paradise we must accustom ourselves to a familiar, humble, affectionate conversation with Him. We must hinder our spirits wandering from Him upon any occasion. We must make our heart a spiritual temple, wherein to adore Him incessantly. We must watch continually over ourselves, that we may not do, nor say, nor think anything that may displease Him. When our minds are thus employed about GOD, suffering will become full of unction and consolation.

I know that to arrive at this state the beginning is very difficult, for we must act purely in faith. But though it is difficult, we know also that we can do all things with the grace of GOD, which He never refuses to them who ask it earnestly. Knock, persevere in knocking, and I answer for it that He will open to you in His due time, and grant you all at once what He has deferred during many years. Adieu! Pray to Him for me, as I pray to Him for you. I hope to see Him quickly.

I am, Yours, &c.

FIFTEENTH LETTER.

To the Same.

GOD knoweth best what is needful for us, and all that He does is for our good. If we knew how much He loves us, we should always be ready to receive equally and with indifference from His Hand the sweet and the bitter: all would please that came from Him. The sorest afflictions never appear intolerable, except when we see them in the wrong light. When we see them as dispensed by the hand of GOD, when we know that it is our loving FATHER who abases and distresses us, our sufferings will lose their bitterness, and become even matter of consolation.

Let all our employment be to *know* GOD: the more one *knows* Him, the more one *desires* to know Him. And as *knowledge* is commonly the measure of *love*, the deeper and more extensive our *knowledge* shall be, the greater will be our *love*: and if our love of GOD were great, we should love Him equally in pains and pleasures.

Let us not content ourselves with loving GOD for the mere sensible favors, how elevated soever, which he has done, or may do us. Such favors, though never so great, cannot bring us so near to Him as faith does in one simple act. Let us seek Him often by faith. He is within us: seek Him not elsewhere. If we do love Him alone, are we not rude, and do we not deserve blame, if we busy ourselves about trifles which do not please and perhaps offend Him. It is to be feared these *trifles* will one day cost us dear.

Let us begin to be devoted to Him in good earnest. Let us cast everything besides out of our hearts. He would possess them alone. Beg this favor of Him. If we do what we can on our parts, we shall soon see that change wrought in us which we aspire after. I cannot thank Him sufficiently for the relaxation He has vouchsafed you. I hope from His mercy the favor to see Him within a few days.[4] Let us pray for one another.

I am, in our LORD, Yours, &c.

---

[4] He took to his bed two days after, and died within the week.

A Simple Biography of Brother Lawrence

Brother Lawrence began life far from the peaceful, wise figure people remember today. He was born around 1614 in Lorraine, a region in eastern France. His birth name was **Nicolas Herman**, and his family was poor. He did not have much schooling, and no one at that time expected him to become a spiritual teacher. He was an ordinary young man living an ordinary life.

As a teenager, he served as a soldier. Life in the army was hard, and during one winter he received a wound that caused him to limp for the rest of his life. This injury followed him everywhere and became part of who he was. After leaving the military, he found work as a household servant, but by his own words, he was clumsy and often broke things. He once laughed at himself, calling his younger self "a great awkward fellow who broke everything."

Yet God was working in him even then.

A Life-Changing Winter Moment

When he was about eighteen, something small but powerful changed his life. One winter day, he saw a bare tree—stripped of its leaves, cold, and lifeless. But he suddenly understood that in spring the tree would bloom again. This simple thought filled him with a deep awareness of God's power and care. That moment opened his heart, and it stayed with him for the rest of his life.

He did not become a monk right away. But the idea that God was alive and active in the world began to shape everything he did.

Entering the Monastery

As he grew older, Nicolas wanted to give his whole life to God. In 1666, he joined the **Carmelite monastery in Paris**. When he entered, he took a new name: **Brother Lawrence of the Resurrection**. He did not enter as a priest or scholar but as a **lay brother**—someone who serves the community through humble, everyday work.

He hoped the monastery would "punish" his clumsiness and teach him discipline. Instead, he found kindness, peace, and a new direction. His main jobs were simple: cooking, cleaning, and repairing sandals. These were not glamorous tasks, but Brother Lawrence believed that even the smallest action could become holy if done with love for God.

    This became the foundation of his whole spiritual life.

Learning to Live With God Every Moment

Brother Lawrence did not learn prayer from long books or special lessons. He learned by trying, failing, and trying again. He began practicing a simple habit:
thinking of God as often as possible, no matter what he was doing.

At first it was difficult. His mind wandered. He fell into doubt. For almost ten years, he struggled with fear that he was not good enough for God. But even in this fear, he kept turning his thoughts back toward God.

And slowly, his heart changed.

Over time, remembering God became natural to him—like breathing. Whether stirring a pot in the noisy kitchen or buying wine for the monastery, he stayed aware of God's presence. People noticed his calmness, his joy, and the peace that seemed to surround him. Many came to him for advice.

He often said:

"The time of business does not differ from the time of prayer."
God is just as close in the kitchen as in the chapel.

His Writings

Brother Lawrence did not try to write a book. After his death in 1691, the monks and friends who knew him gathered his **conversations** and **letters**. These were published as *The Practice of the Presence of God*, the book you are now reading.

His writings are simple, honest, and gentle.
He does not preach. He shares.

The Final Years

Brother Lawrence lived to about eighty years old. Even in sickness, he remained peaceful and joyful, saying he trusted God with everything. When he died, he left no great achievements in the world—no buildings, no positions, no theological systems.

But he left something far greater:
an example of how an ordinary life can become extraordinary through love, awareness, and simplicity.

*His life shows that **anyone**
—no matter their education, background, or job—*
can learn to live close to God.

Life of Brother Lawrence

Year	Event
1614	Nicolas Herman (Brother Lawrence) is born in Lorraine, France.
Early 1630s	Serves as a soldier; injured during winter, leaving a lifelong limp.
Mid-1630s	Experiences a spiritual awakening after seeing a bare winter tree.
1640s–1650s	Works as a household servant; continues seeking a deeper life with God.
1666	Enters the Carmelite monastery in Paris; becomes Brother Lawrence of the Resurrection.
1666–1670	Assigned simple tasks: cooking, cleaning, repairing sandals. Begins practicing continual awareness of God.
1670s	Known for unusual peace and joy; many seek his advice on prayer and presence.
1670s–1680s	Conversations with Brother Lawrence recorded by friends; he writes letters offering guidance.
1691	Brother Lawrence dies around age 80.
1692	First edition of *The Practice of the Presence of God* published by Joseph de Beaufort.
1700s–1800s	The book spreads across Europe; translated into English, German, and Dutch.
1895	English edition published (the edition used for this volume).
1900s–2000s	Book becomes a worldwide spiritual classic, loved by Christians and non-Christians alike.
Today	A new generation discovers Brother Lawrence's message of simplicity, peace, and daily awareness of God.

A Practical Manual for Daily Life
HOW TO PRACTICE GOD'S PRESENCE TODAY

What It Means to "Practice God's Presence"

To "practice the presence of God" means learning to live your daily life with a steady awareness that God is near—right in the middle of your work, your thoughts, your worries, and your rest. It is not about feeling holy or perfect. It is not about trying harder or praying longer. It is simply about **remembering**.

Remembering that God is here.
Remembering that you are not alone.
Remembering that you can turn your heart toward Him at any moment.

Brother Lawrence discovered that this simple habit changed everything. Tasks felt lighter. Stress felt smaller. Joy felt deeper. He became more patient, more peaceful, and more loving—not because he escaped from life, but because he carried God with him *into* life.

This manual is designed to help you do the same in today's busy world. It offers small steps that anyone can follow, whether you are a student, a parent, a worker, or someone searching for peace.

The First Step:
A Heart That Wants God

Before any method or technique, Brother Lawrence teaches us that the most important thing is **desire**.
A heart that wants God, even imperfectly, is enough.

Start With Honesty

You do not need to pretend.
You do not need to impress God.
You do not need to be "good enough."

Simply admit:
"God, I want to know You better. Help me begin."

That one sentence is the doorway.

Begin Where You Are

You may feel:

- distracted
- stressed
- spiritually dry
- unsure what you believe
- guilty or unworthy
- busy and tired

None of that disqualifies you. Brother Lawrence said he began his journey feeling weak, sinful, and easily distracted. What mattered was that he kept trying.

Your life—exactly as it is—is the starting point.

Make a Gentle Resolution

A "resolution" is not a strict rule. It's a gentle promise made with love.

Say something like:
"I will try to remember God as often as I can today."

That is all.

You do not need to pray perfectly.
You do not need to think spiritual thoughts all day.
You are simply opening your door a little wider.

Turning Ordinary Moments Into Prayer

One of Brother Lawrence's greatest insights is that **ordinary life is full of opportunities to meet God**.

You do not need extra time—just extra awareness.

Short, Simple Heart-Prayers

Brother Lawrence used tiny prayers throughout the day. You can do the same:

- "Lord, be with me."
- "God, I'm listening."
- "Help me."
- "Thank You."
- "I trust You."

These prayers take **one breath**.
You can whisper them anywhere:

- in the car
- at work
- while washing dishes
- in a difficult conversation

They reconnect you to the Presence.

Using Your Body as a Reminder

Pick one common action and let it remind you of God.

For example:

- When you open a door → "Lord, open my heart."
- When you wash your hands → "Cleanse me."
- When you drink water → "Fill me with Your peace."
- When you sit down → "Be with me here."

These habits slowly train your mind to return to God naturally.

Bringing God Into Work

Brother Lawrence discovered God in the noisy kitchen. You can discover God:

- in your office
- at school
- in meetings
- while caring for children
- during chores

Say:
"This work is for You, Lord. Stay with me as I do it."

This turns work into worship.

Turning Stress Into Prayer

When you feel anxious or overwhelmed:

1. Breathe slowly.
2. Say, "God, I give this to You."
3. Imagine handing the problem to Him.

This grounds your spirit and reduces fear.

Quieting the Mind in a Loud World

Brother Lawrence lived in the 1600s, without phones, notifications, traffic, or constant news. But he still struggled with wandering thoughts. He understood the human mind well.

Today the world is louder than ever, so our minds need extra care.

Here are simple ways to create inner quiet.

One-Minute Stillness

Try this once or twice a day:

1. Sit or stand comfortably.
2. Close your eyes if you can.
3. Take one slow breath in and out.
4. Say softly: "God, You are here."
5. Rest for a moment in that truth.

This resets your heart.

Letting Thoughts Pass

When distractions come, don't fight them.

Instead:

- Notice them
- Let them go
- Gently return your attention to God

Brother Lawrence said that when his mind wandered, he simply turned back to God "with greater trust" each time.

He treated distractions like a child returning home— never with anger, always with welcome.

Reducing Mental Clutter

Here are small habits that make presence easier:

- Limit screen time before bed
- Step outside for a moment of fresh air
- Keep your favorite short prayer near you
- Take small pauses during the day
- Practice gratitude to stay grounded

Quiet minds notice God more easily.

Making Space in Your Heart

Sometimes our hearts feel crowded with:

- fear
- comparison
- busyness
- worry
- guilt

Give those things to God by naming them:

"Lord, I'm worried about ____. I place it in Your hands."

When you let go of what you're carrying, you make room for God's peace.

Practicing God's Presence in Relationships

We often think prayer happens only when we are alone, but Brother Lawrence believed that **loving others is part of loving God**. When we bring God into our relationships, we become more patient, gentle, and present.

Here are simple ways to practice:

Listen With Love

- When speaking with someone:
  - Slow down
  - Look at them
- Listen without planning your reply

Before they speak, whisper in your heart:
"Lord, help me see this person as You see them."

This turns conversations into moments of grace.

Bless People Quietly

In your mind, you can pray:
"God, give them peace."
"Lord, help them today."
"Strengthen them."

This builds compassion and softens frustration.

Bring God Into Conflict

When tension rises:

- o Pause
- o Breathe

- Pray: "Lord, calm my heart. Help me respond with kindness."

This prayer may save a friendship, protect a marriage, or soften a difficult exchange at work.

Serve With a Willing Heart

Brother Lawrence said even simple tasks can become holy when done for love of God.

Try this:

- o Make a meal → "Lord, bless this food."
- o Help your child → "Help me show Your patience."
- o Care for the sick → "Be near them."

Small acts become spiritual moments.

Presence in Suffering, Doubt, and Dry Seasons

Life is not always peaceful. We face:

- loss
- fear
- pain
- disappointment
- spiritual dryness

Brother Lawrence did too. He struggled for nearly **10 years** with fear, guilt, and doubt before he found peace.

Here's how to practice presence in hard times.

Be Honest With God

God does not ask for perfect emotions.
Say:
"Lord, I'm hurting."
"God, I don't understand."
"Lord, stay with me."

Honesty is prayer.

Pain Does Not Push God Away

Brother Lawrence wrote that some of his closest moments with God came during his darkest times. He believed God draws near to the brokenhearted.

When suffering hits, pray:
"Walk with me through this."

When You Feel Nothing

Some days you may feel spiritually empty. That is normal. Even the saints experienced it.

In those seasons:

- keep praying simple prayers
- keep turning your heart to God
- keep trusting that He is near

Presence is not a feeling—it is a choice made again and again.

Use Breath as Anchoring

Slowly inhale: "God, You are here."
Slowly exhale: "I give You my burden."

This helps calm the mind and return the heart to God.

Remember:
Growth Is Slow

Just like a tree grows quietly underground before sprouting, spiritual growth often happens unseen. Suffering softens the soil of the heart.

In time, peace will rise again.

Practicing Presence in Work, Creativity, and Parenting

Brother Lawrence found God in the kitchen.
You can find God anywhere—
in the studio, at your job, in your home, or while raising children.

Practicing Presence at Work

Before you start your day, pray:
"Lord, work through me."

During your tasks, say:
"Help me do this well."
"Give me strength."
"Let this honor You."

Even routine work becomes meaningful when God is invited into it.

Practicing Presence for Creative People

Writers, musicians, designers, and artists can pray: "Create through me."

Let God into:

- o   your ideas
- o   your decisions
- o   your inspiration
- o   your frustration

Offer your craft to Him, and your creativity becomes prayer.

Practicing Presence at Home

Home is where distractions are strongest, but it is also where God can be found most deeply.

- o   Hug your children → "Bless them, Lord."
- o   Pay bills → "Give us wisdom."
- o   Clean the house → "Thank You for this home."
- o   Eat meals → "Thank You for this food."

Ordinary life becomes holy.

Practicing Presence When Caring for Others

Whether caring for children, elders, or patients:

- Look them in the eyes
- Speak gently
- See Christ in their need

Pray:
"Lord, love them through me."

This kind of presence leaves a mark that lasts.

Presence Without Perfection

Many people give up on prayer because they believe they fail too often. Brother Lawrence understood this deeply. He said the spiritual life is made of **small beginnings** repeated many times.

Expect Distractions

Your mind will wander.
You will forget to pray.
You may go hours without thinking of God.

This is normal.

When you notice, gently return to God:
"Here I am again."

That return *is* the practice.

Drop the Burden of Guilt

God is not disappointed in you.
He is delighted each time you turn back to Him.

Brother Lawrence taught that God is more honored
by one honest return than by hours of forced devotion.

Focus on Faithfulness, Not Perfection

Spiritual growth is not about doing everything right. It is about:

- showing up
- trying again
- trusting God
- keeping your heart open

You cannot force presence.
You can only welcome it.

Celebrate Small Victories

Did you remember God once today?
That is success.

Did you pray for one minute?
Success.

Did you turn to God in a stressful moment?
Success.

Small steps build a lifelong habit.

A 30-Day Practice Guide

Here is a simple, gentle plan to help you
build the habit of God's presence.
Each day uses one small action that takes only a few minutes.

Week 1 — Awareness

- **Day 1:** "God, You are here." Say it once in the morning.
- **Day 2:** Use one short prayer throughout the day.
- **Day 3:** Pause for one minute of stillness.
- **Day 4:** Thank God for three small things.
- **Day 5:** Say a short prayer before each task.
- **Day 6:** Take a slow walk or breath—"Be with me."
- **Day 7:** Review the week. Celebrate one moment of presence.

Week 2 — Turning Moments Into Prayer

- **Day 8:** Choose a "reminder action" (door, water, sitting).
- **Day 9:** Whisper blessings for others.
- **Day 10:** Pray during a simple chore.
- **Day 11:** Invite God into your work.
- **Day 12:** Use breath-prayer during stress.
- **Day 13:** Spend five minutes in quiet gratitude.
- **Day 14:** Review and reflect.

Week 3 — Deepening Trust

- **Day 15:** Tell God one worry.
- **Day 16:** Pray for someone difficult.
- **Day 17:** Practice listening in a conversation.
- **Day 18:** Use a short Scripture or phrase.
- **Day 19:** Offer your frustrations to God.
- **Day 20:** Meditate on "God is with me."
- **Day 21:** Review your heart.

Week 4 — Living Daily Presence

- **Day 22:** Bring God into meals.
- **Day 23:** Invite God into your creativity.
- **Day 24:** Serve someone with love.
- **Day 25:** Pray over your relationships.
- **Day 26:** Let go of one burden.
- **Day 27:** Thank God for your life today.
- **Day 28:** Sit in quiet for two minutes.
- **Day 29:** Pray: "Make Your home in me."
- **Day 30:** Look back. Notice the change.

Spiritual habits grow slowly—but steadily.

Closing Reflection:
A Life With God

At the end of all these practices is something simple:
a life with God woven into every moment.

Brother Lawrence did not become a saint overnight. He grew day by day, step by step, by turning to God again and again with love.

You can do the same.

Let your daily tasks become prayers.
Let your struggles become conversations.
Let your joys become gratitude.
Let your whole life become a place where God is welcome.

The goal is not perfection.
The goal is presence.

Every moment, God invites you closer.
Every moment, you can say "yes."

May this practice bring peace to your heart, strength to your days, and a gentle awareness of God's love in all things.

Spiritual Minimalism:
Living Simply With God

In our modern world, people collect many things—ideas, habits, possessions, apps, goals, worries, and expectations. Our minds often feel crowded, our emotions overloaded, and our souls tired. Many feel that life has become too full, yet strangely empty.

Brother Lawrence offers a surprising answer to this problem: **spiritual minimalism.**
Not minimalism in décor or lifestyle, but minimalism of the *heart*.

Spiritual minimalism means removing what does not help you love God, so your heart has room for what truly matters: peace, presence, trust, and love.

This section explains how Brother Lawrence practiced this, and how you can too.

The Heart Has Limited Space

Just like a room, the heart can only hold so much.
When it is filled with:

- fear
- anxiety
- comparison
- frustration
- constant noise
- too many goals
- too much information

there is very little room left for peace.

Brother Lawrence understood this. He once wrote that unnecessary thoughts "spoil all" because they pull the soul away from God. By learning to let go of extra noise, he created a quiet space inside himself where God could dwell.

Spiritual simplicity creates spiritual space.

Letting Go of the Unnecessary

Spiritual minimalism is not about owning fewer things—it is about carrying fewer burdens.

You can practice this by letting go of:

- repeating worries
- regrets you cannot change
- the need to control everything
- harsh self-judgment
- jealousy or resentment
- the pressure to be perfect
- constant mental clutter

Each time you release something, you make room for God to enter.

Try saying:
"Lord, I give this up so I can hold on to You."

Choosing What Matters Most

A simple spiritual life is not an empty one—it is a focused one.

Brother Lawrence chose only three priorities:

1. **Remember God.**
2. **Trust God.**
3. **Love God in small, daily actions.**

Everything else was secondary.

You can practice the same by asking:

- Does this thought bring me closer to God?
- Does this habit help me or distract me?
  - Is this worry necessary?
  - Is this extra, or essential?

This helps your soul stay centered.

Bringing Stillness Into a Busy World

Stillness is not about stopping your life. It is about carrying peace inside your life.

To practice:

- Take small pauses during the day
- Breathe before reacting
- Pray simple prayers
- Do one thing at a time
- Leave room for rest
- Step away from constant screens and noise

Stillness makes space for God's voice.

Simplicity in Prayer

Prayer does not need to be long or complicated.

Brother Lawrence prayed with simple words:

- "Lord, I am Yours."
- "Help me."
- "I trust You."
- "Thank You, God."

These short prayers are powerful because they come from the heart. They clear away extra words and leave only what is real.

Spiritual minimalism brings clarity to prayer.

Simplicity in Service and Work

Brother Lawrence believed that small acts done with love matter more than big acts done with pride. He found holiness in:

- cooking food
- sweeping floors
- repairing sandals
- serving others

When you simplify your intentions—doing things for love, not praise—your actions become peaceful and meaningful.

A simple task done with God becomes holy.

Making Room for God in Daily Life

Here is a small practice you can use each morning:

Morning Clearing Prayer

"Lord, remove from my heart anything that keeps me from You. Make space inside me for peace, love, and Your presence."

Then sit for 30 seconds and breathe.

This is spiritual housekeeping.

The Freedom of a Simple Soul

When you practice spiritual minimalism, you begin to feel lighter.
Your mind becomes clearer.
Your emotions calmer.
Your decisions simpler.
Your connection with God stronger.

You realize you don't need:

- constant success
- constant stimulation
- constant approval
- constant activity

Instead, you need God—steady, near, faithful, and present.

In spiritual minimalism, the soul learns that **less is not a loss.**
Less is **freedom.**

Brother Lawrence's Message for Today

If Brother Lawrence walked into our world, filled with notifications, ads, schedules, and noise, he might simply smile and say:

"You are carrying too much. Put some of it down.
Make room for God.
Live simply.
Love deeply.
Be present."

That is the heart of spiritual minimalism.

And it is available to you—right now, in this moment.

The Christian Home as a Place of Daily Liturgy

Many people think worship happens only in a church. But throughout Christian history, the home has been seen as the first and most important place where faith is lived. You do not need stained glass, pews, or a pulpit for spiritual life to take shape. You simply need a willing heart and a home—no matter its size, condition, or noise level.

Your home can become a place of **daily liturgy**, meaning small everyday actions that center your life around God.

The Home as Holy Ground

A Christian home is not perfect. It is not quiet all the time. It is not free of disagreements. A Christian home is simply a place where God is invited into ordinary life.

This can happen:

- at the table
- by the bed
- during chores
- while getting ready for work
- while caring for children
- during moments of rest

Each one becomes an opportunity for presence.

Small Rituals Create Stability

You don't need long rituals—small ones work beautifully:

- a short prayer before meals
- a whispered blessing before sleep
- a Scripture verse on the wall
- a peaceful corner for reflection
- a quiet moment in the morning

These simple habits shape the rhythm of the home and help everyone feel grounded and cared for.

Love Makes a Home Sacred

Brother Lawrence taught that small acts done with love are as holy as great acts done on a stage.
This means:

- folding laundry with patience
- comforting a child
- forgiving quickly
- offering kindness
- treating each person with dignity

When love is present, God is present.

Turning Chores Into Moments With God

A home constantly needs maintenance. Instead of seeing chores as interruptions, you can use them as prayers:

- washing dishes → "Lord, wash my heart."
- sweeping floors → "Sweep away my worries."
- cooking → "Bless those who will eat this."

Simple work becomes spiritual practice.

The Goal Is Not Perfection—It's Presence

A Christian home doesn't need to look "religious." It simply needs people who want God near.

With small daily habits, your home becomes more than a building. It becomes a place where faith grows naturally—like light entering through open windows.

Why the Psalms Were Considered Medicine for the Soul

For thousands of years, people have turned to the Psalms during times of joy, fear, grief, and hope. Monks recited them daily. Families memorized them. Soldiers carried them into battle. Even today, people who do not attend church still read the Psalms for comfort.

Why? Because the Psalms speak the full language of the human heart.

The Psalms Speak Honestly

Unlike polished prayers, the Psalms include:

- anger
- fear
- doubt
- sadness
- joy
- hope
- gratitude

They allow you to bring your whole self before God. Honesty is healing.

The Psalms Remind Us of God's Care

Many Psalms were written during danger or uncertainty. They show a God who:

- protects
- listens
- rescues
- guides
- comforts

This brings emotional steadiness in difficult times.

Psalms Calm the Mind

Reading a Psalm slowly:

- slows your breathing
- gives structure to your thoughts
- replaces fear with faith
- helps the mind settle

This is why the Psalms are often used to help with anxiety and grief.

The Psalms Create Community

Families, churches, and entire nations have used the Psalms together. They help people feel connected when words are hard to find.

When you pray a Psalm, you join a long line of believers who have prayed those same words for centuries.

The Psalms Invite God Into Real Life

Psalm prayers are short, simple, and deeply human:

- "The Lord is my shepherd."
- "God is our refuge and strength."
- "Create in me a clean heart."

These lines settle the heart and become spiritual medicine—reminding us that we are not alone.

Why Spoken Blessings Carry Healing Power

Across Christian history, the spoken word has been seen as powerful—
not because of magic, but because of meaning, intention, and the presence of God.

Words shape hearts.
Words calm fear.
Words give strength.
Words guide the soul.

Brother Lawrence knew this, and Christian traditions around the world have practiced spoken blessings as a form of daily healing.

Words Carry Weight

A kind word can lift the spirit.
A harsh word can wound it.

This is why Scripture teaches:
"Life and death are in the power of the tongue."

Spoken blessings choose life.

Blessings Bring God Into the Moment

A blessing is simply speaking good over someone in God's name:

- "God be with you."
- "May the Lord give you peace."
- "May God strengthen you today."

These words invite God's comfort and care.

Blessings Create Connection

When you bless someone, you:

- pay attention to them
- care for their heart
- offer encouragement
- share God's love

It builds community and deepens relationships.

Blessings Calm the Mind and Body

Hearing a blessing helps people:

- o breathe slower
- o feel supported
- o experience peace
- o release anxiety

Parents use blessings before bed.
Friends use blessings during struggle.
Spouses use blessings before difficult days.

This is true healing.

Blessings Help Us Practice Presence

When you bless someone:

- o you slow down
- o you look at them with love
- o you become aware of God
- o you turn the moment holy

This is exactly the spirit of Brother Lawrence:
God is present, and love makes Him known.

A Simple Guide to Carmelite & Monastic Mysticism

Interior Prayer, Ancient Practices, and the Way of Presence

Brother Lawrence lived in a Carmelite monastery,
a place shaped by centuries of Christian prayer. The Carmelites focus
on **interior prayer**,
a gentle way of being with God that does not depend on long words
or complex rituals.
Their goal is simple:
to love God with the heart, in quiet, constant awareness.

You do not need to be a monk to practice these things.
You do not need vows, a robe, or a life in a cloister.
These teachings can help *anyone* walk more closely with God in daily
life.

Below is a short, friendly guide to the traditions that shaped
Brother Lawrence.

Interior Prayer
(Heart Prayer)

Interior prayer is the quiet turning of the heart toward God. It is not reciting many words.
It is not trying to "achieve" something. It is sitting with God inwardly,
like resting beside someone who loves you.

For the Carmelites, interior prayer meant:

- being still for a moment
- remembering God is near
- loving Him silently
- listening more than speaking

Brother Lawrence practiced this all day long—
while cooking, cleaning, or resting.

Apophatic vs. Kataphatic Prayer

These two ancient styles help explain different ways people pray.

Kataphatic Prayer
(Prayer With Images and Words)

- Uses Scripture, pictures, emotions, or imagination
- Examples: meditating on Jesus's life, praying with a Psalm, imagining Gospel scenes

This type of prayer is warm, emotional, and expressive.

Apophatic Prayer
(Prayer Beyond Images and Words)

- Simple awareness of God without many thoughts
- Letting go of images and emotions
- Sitting in quiet trust

This is closer to Brother Lawrence's way—just being with God.

Most people use both forms at different times. Neither is better; both help the soul grow.

Lectio Divina
(*Sacred Reading*)

Lectio Divina is an old monastic practice for reading Scripture slowly and prayerfully.

It has four gentle steps:

1. **Read** a short passage (like a verse or two).
2. **Reflect** on a word or phrase that touches your heart.
3. **Respond** to God with a short prayer.
4. **Rest** quietly in His presence.

This practice trains the mind to slow down and the heart to open.

The Cloud of Unknowing
(*English Mysticism*)

In the 1300s, an anonymous writer created a short book called *The Cloud of Unknowing*. It teaches that God is known not by thinking a lot, but by loving a lot.

The book says:

- God is too great to understand fully
- The mind often gets in the way
- Love reaches God better than thought

Brother Lawrence lived this. He said that simply turning the heart toward God brings us closer than trying to "figure God out."

Hesychasm and the Jesus Prayer
(Eastern Christian Practice)

Hesychasm is an ancient prayer tradition from the Eastern Orthodox Church.
Its main tool is the **Jesus Prayer**:

"Lord Jesus Christ, Son of God, have mercy on me."

People pray it slowly, with their breath, again and again until it becomes part of the heart.

Hesychasts believed:

- prayer should be constant
- the mind should rest in the heart
- peace comes from gentle repetition

This is very close to Brother Lawrence's "continual turning toward God."

How All These Traditions Point to Presence

Though they come from different places and time periods, all these practices share the same truth:

God is near.
The heart can return to Him at any moment.
Quiet love brings the soul into His presence.

You do not need to become a monk, leave your job, or change your whole life.
Presence is possible **right where you are**, in the middle of your day.

These paths simply teach you how to slow down, breathe, and remember God's love—
just as Brother Lawrence did.

Annotated Glossary of Spiritual Terms

This glossary uses simple definitions with short explanations so readers of all backgrounds can understand Brother Lawrence's language.

Grace

A word with **two** major meanings in **Christian** history:

1. Monastic Definition

Grace is God's gentle help—
His presence, peace, and strength given freely.

It is like sunlight: constant, warm, steady, even when unnoticed.

2. Protestant Definition

Grace is God's unearned favor—
His forgiveness, mercy, and acceptance through Christ.

Not something earned, but freely given.

Both meanings point to the same truth:
God helps, God forgives, God supports, God draws near.

Recollection

Gently gathering your scattered thoughts and turning them back toward God. *Life pulls the mind in many directions. "Recollection" brings it home to God again.*

Interior Silence

A quiet state of heart where you are less distracted and more aware of God.
Not outward silence—inner stillness.
It helps you hear God without noise from worries or fears.

Devotion

Loving God with sincerity, faithfulness, and attention.
Not dramatic emotion—steady love.
Devotion is the root attitude that makes prayer natural.

Continual Prayer

Short, frequent moments of prayer throughout the day.
Brother Lawrence did this constantly—
simple words, simple love.
It keeps the heart connected to God in real time.

Spiritual Habit

A small, repeated action that shapes your spiritual life.
Examples: a short prayer, a morning pause, a blessing before meals. *Habits slowly transform the heart without force.*

Meditation
(Christian)

Slow, thoughtful reflection on Scripture, God's love, or Christ's life. Different from Eastern styles—this focuses on **God, not the** *self.*
It deepens understanding and softens the heart.

Solitude

Time alone with God.
Not loneliness—**intentional quiet**.
Helps the soul rest and hear God more clearly.

Presence

Awareness of **God** in the moment.
*This is Brother Lawrence's central teaching—**God is here, and your heart can live in that awareness**.*

Surrender

Giving God your worries, fears, and plans, *trusting Him fully.*
***Surrender** brings **peace** and **frees** the **mind** from **heavy burdens**.*

Love of God

A gentle, steady affection for God that **grows** *through* **daily practice**.
***Love**—not fear—is the center of Christian life.*

Reflective Questions for the Reader's Heart

Sit with me now—slowly, honestly—almost like we are gathered in a quiet room with warm light and no hurry.
I will not lecture,
and you need not perform.
Let us think together.

We have read a book that whispers instead of shouts.
A book that suggests God is not only found in holy places but in the soft hum of ordinary life.

So I ask you:
*Where does your heart wander when the world is loud?
And what would it take to bring your awareness back to the Presence that already sits beside you?*

Brother Lawrence failed often, yet returned gently.
No shame, no ceremony—
just a turning.

So consider:
*When you drift away—into worry, anger, or habit—what draws you back?
What might a gentle return look like for you, without punishment or pressure?*

There are seasons when prayer feels thin and God feels quiet.

Think with me:
Is silence always absence, or could silence sometimes be invitation?

What truths have you learned in the moments that hurt the most?

Brother Lawrence carried fewer thoughts so he could carry more peace.
Not emptiness—clarity.

Reflect with me:
What unnecessary weights does your heart carry?

What could you set down—not out of avoidance, but out of trust?

Every person who crosses our path becomes a teacher—if we are willing to see them.

Ask yourself:
Where have you seen God hide inside another person's need, weakness, or kindness?

How might your way of listening change if you believed each conversation could be holy?

The kitchen became Brother Lawrence's cathedral.
The pots and pans were his icons.
He sanctified the ordinary by offering it to God.

So examine:
What part of your daily labor is waiting to become prayer?

What task—however humble—could become sacred with the right intention?

Spiritual growth is rarely fast.
Trust unfolds slowly, like dawn.

Consider:
Where do you hesitate to trust God?

What would trust look like if it were not a feeling, but a steady decision?

We often rush past one another without seeing the soul behind the face.

Let me ask you:
Who in your life needs a quieter, gentler version of you?

What would it look like to make your presence a blessing in their day?

Grace is more than pardon.
It is God's steady nearness—
the light that stays even when we forget to look.

Ask yourself:
When has grace found you unexpectedly?

How might you make room for grace to find you again?

Brother Lawrence teaches us not to escape life, but to sanctify it.
Not to seek new places, but new awareness.

So finally:
What small practices could help your life itself become a prayer?

How might you carry God with you after these pages close?

There is a version of you that God sees clearly—even when you cannot.

Sit with this:
Who are you becoming when you are most true, most honest, and most unafraid?

What part of that person is asking to be welcomed now, not later?

Not every truth arrives through understanding; some arrive through surrender.

So ask gently:
What mysteries in your life invite you not to explain them, but to bow before them?

Where is humility asking to take the place of certainty?

Light often works in silence— healing, shaping, guiding without spectacle.

Reflect on this:
Where has quiet goodness shaped you more deeply than loud instruction ever could?

What quiet goodness might you offer the world in return?

Wounds do not always disappear; sometimes they transform us.

Consider:
What places of hurt in your life are beginning to glow instead of bleed?

What would it mean to honor the healing already at work in you?

Every ending is also an entrance; every circle closes only to open again.

Ask yourself:
What truth from these pages follows you into tomorrow?

And how will you walk differently now that you know Presence walks with you?

I pose these questions not as a preacher, nor as a scholar, nor even as a guide—but as someone sitting beside you, exploring the same mysteries. The answers belong to you, and they will deepen over time.

A Closing Meditation

There are books that speak with thunder, and there are books that speak with a whisper. Brother Lawrence chose the whisper, and somehow it echoes louder across the centuries than most sermons ever have. As I reach the end of this book, I find myself not full of ideas but full of quiet. A gentle quiet, the kind that invites the heart to breathe again after carrying more than it should.

What touches me most about Brother Lawrence is not his wisdom but his humanity. He limped. He dropped things. He doubted. He feared he wasn't good enough. And yet he discovered God, not by rising above his humanity but by entering it more honestly. That gives me hope. It tells me that God walks best with those who walk slowly.

When I look at my own life—its responsibilities, its ambitions, its noise—I realize how often I chase God through extraordinary means while He waits for me in ordinary ones. I look for God in the big decisions, the major turning points, the rare flashes of clarity. But God waits for me in the hallway between errands, in the stillness before words form, in the breath I take without thinking. It humbles me to admit that for years I walked past Him while searching for Him.

Brother Lawrence reminds me that prayer is not something I begin; it is something I join. God is already speaking. God is already present. God has already gone ahead of me into the day. My role is simply to wake up to that Presence. This realization changes how I read Scripture, how I work, and how I move through relationships. It changes how I carry my burdens. It even changes how I breathe.

There have been seasons where I felt spiritually dry, where prayer felt like speaking into a cold room. I used to think that silence meant distance. Now I see that silence can mean invitation. God sometimes clears the inner noise so that I may learn to rest instead of strive. In those seasons, I learn the power of returning—returning to God without shame, without performance, without the pressure to feel something holy. Just returning.

This returning applies to my failures as well. The older I get, the more aware I am of the things I cannot fix—moments I mishandled, people I failed, dreams I delayed. But Brother Lawrence teaches me that guilt does not honor God; honesty does. I can bring my broken places to Him, and He meets me with mercy instead of measurement. He does not count how many times I fall. He celebrates how many times I come back.

Perhaps the deepest lesson I've learned through this book is the sacredness of small things. Greatness is not what opens the door to God. Love does. Love in simple acts. Love in quiet service. Love in the way I speak, listen, forgive, and show patience. Love in the way I choose presence over hurry. Holiness hides itself in the ordinary, waiting to be noticed.

This awareness changes how I see the people around me. Every person becomes a reminder that God is near. In a world filled with division and noise, remembering God in others becomes an anchor. I listen differently. I speak more gently. I carry fewer weapons inside my words. Brother Lawrence's practice softens the heart in ways doctrine alone cannot.

What also moves me is how universal this path is. It is Christian at its core, but it resonates far beyond any one tradition. Every faith has a way of quieting the heart. Every soul hungers for peace. Every human being knows what it feels like to be overwhelmed. This practice meets people where they are, without demanding that they become someone else first.

As I close this reflection, I find myself grateful—not only for Brother Lawrence but for the God he teaches us to see. A God who does not hide in temples or towers. A God who does not wait for perfect prayers. A God who steps into kitchens, workplaces, commutes, bedrooms, offices, cars, and crowded minds. A God who is content to walk with us at our pace. A God who wants to be found.

If there is one gift this book gives, it is this: the grace of awareness.

Awareness that God is already here.
Awareness that love is stronger than fear.
Awareness that our returning is always welcome.
Awareness that holiness is woven into the ordinary.
Awareness that a quiet heart can hold great things.

May the presence Brother Lawrence practiced
become your companion.
May your days become lighter, your choices gentler,
your spirit steadier.
And may you discover, again and again,
that God is not far from you—
He is closer than your next breath.

May the quiet wisdom of these pages settle softly into your life.
May the God who walked beside Brother Lawrence walk beside you
in every moment that follows—
not in thunder, not in spectacle,
but in the simple grace of being present.

May your home become a place of peace,
your work a place of purpose,
your rest a place of renewal.
May ordinary tasks turn holy in your hands,
and may small acts of love bloom into sacred offerings.

When your mind wanders,
may you return gently.
When your heart grows weary,
may you find strength in God's nearness.
When your path feels uncertain,
may you remember that Presence is a light
that never dims,
never flees,
never forgets you.

May grace greet you in the morning,
walk with you through the day,
and keep watch over you in the night.
May the peace of Christ rest upon your spirit
like a warm mantle,
steadying your breath,
quieting your fears,
and reminding you that you are held.

May you discover God in the simple and the ordinary.
May you hear Him in silence,
feel Him in stillness,
and find Him in the spaces you once thought empty.

And as you practice this Presence—
slowly, softly, faithfully—
may you become a living prayer,
a quiet flame,
and a gentle light for others.

Go now in peace,
carrying the Presence that carries you.

Also Hear These Works in the Voice of Dennis Logan

Over the past decade I have devoted thousands of hours to recording sacred texts, apocrypha, and esoteric classics.

If **The God Who Is Near** spoke to you,
you can continue the journey through our expanding library of works in scripture, apocrypha, esoterica, philosophy, folklore, mysticism, and political thought.

You will find many of the texts referenced in our Legitimate Sacred Texts Catalog, our Legitimate Esoteric & Occult Corpus, and even the works that inform our Grand Catalog of Hoaxes and Pseudepigrapha— all read, rendered, and reissued with care.

To explore the complete catalogue of **100+ audiobooks**, from the Bible and Koran to grimoires, mystic treatises, revolutionary texts, and the great currents of world literature:

Search "Dennis Logan" on Audible.

New titles are released monthly as part of Penemue Media's ongoing commitment to clarity, preservation, and the restoration of our shared intellectual lineage.

Scripture, Apocrypha & Ancient Texts

- *The Universal Bible of the Protestant, Catholic, Orthodox, Ethiopic, Syriac, and Samaritan Church*
- *Lost Books of the Bible: The Great Rejected Texts*
- *The Book of Jasher*
- *Book of Enoch, Jubilees, Jasher & The Book of Giants: The Complete Scriptures of Nephilim & Fallen Angels*
- *The Books of Enoch and The Book of Giants (featuring 1, 2, and 3 Enoch with the Aramaic and Manichean Giants texts)*
- *The Book of Jubilees: The Little Genesis, The Apocalypse of Moses*
- *The First and Second Books of Adam and Eve*
- *The Pentautech: The 5 Books of Moses*
- *The War Scroll: The War of the Sons of Light Against the Sons of Darkness*
- *The Kebra Nagast: The Glory of the Kings*
- *The Book of the Bee: The Syriac Text*
- *The Holy Piby: The Blackman's Bible*
- *The Gospel of Nicodemus, the Acts of Pilate and the Harrowing of Hell*
- *The Books of Jasher*

Magick & Occult Classics

- *The Universal One: Walter Russell's Foundational Mind-Centered Electromagnetic Universe Treatise-Exact Facsimile with Full Illustrations*
- *Paradoxes of the Highest Science*
- *Aradia: The Gospel of the Witches*
- *The Magus or Celestial Intelligencer: A Modern Rendering of the 1801 Edition*
- *The Book of the Sacred Magic of Abramelin the Mage: A Modern Rendering of the 15th Century Grimoire*
- *The Lesser Key of Solomon: A Modern Rendering of the 17th Century Grimoire*
- *The Greater Key of Solomon: A Modern Rendering of the 15th Century Grimoire*
- *An Outline of Occult Science: A Modern Edition*
- *A Textbook of Theosophy*
- *The Prodigal – Wow A Long Lost Friend Returns*

Gnostic, Mystical & Esoteric Studies

- *Banned from the Bible*
- *The Secret Gospel of Mark*
- *The Gospel of Barnabas*
- *The Gospel of Judas: The Man, His History, His Story*
- *The Aquarian Gospel of Jesus the Christ*
- *The Gnostic Gospels of Philip, Mary Magdalene, and Thomas*
- *The Gnostic Scriptures*
- *An Advanced Lesson in Gnosticism*
- *The Apocryphon of John: A Gnostic Gospel*
- *The Secret Teachings of All Ages*
- *The Kybalion, Tablet of Hermes & Emerald Tablets*
- *Thought-Forms*
- *The Initiates of the Flame*
- *Golden Verses of Pythagoras & Other Pythagorean Fragments*
- *Science of Breath*
- *The Way of Initiation: How to Attain Knowledge of the Higher Worlds: A Modern Edition*
- *The Education of Children: From the Standpoint of Theosophy: A Modern Edition*

Original Works by Dennis Logan

- *The Panerotic Sutras of Master Stryfe*
- *The Apocatastasis of Enoch*
- *The Testament of Samson*
- *White Ancestors, Black Scripture*

Also Hear These Works in the Voice of Dennis Logan

Over the past decade I have devoted thousands of hours to recording sacred texts, apocrypha, and esoteric classics.

If **The God Who Is Near** spoke to you,
you can continue the journey through our expanding library of works in scripture, apocrypha, esoterica, philosophy, folklore, mysticism, and political thought.

You will find many of the texts referenced in our Legitimate Sacred Texts Catalog, our Legitimate Esoteric & Occult Corpus, and even the works that inform our Grand Catalog of Hoaxes and Pseudepigrapha— all read, rendered, and reissued with care.

To explore the complete catalogue of **100+ audiobooks**, from the Bible and Koran to grimoires, mystic treatises, revolutionary texts, and the great currents of world literature:

Search "Dennis Logan" on Audible.

New titles are released monthly as part of Penemue Media's ongoing commitment to clarity, preservation, and the restoration of our shared intellectual lineage.

Scripture, Apocrypha & Ancient Texts

- *The Universal Bible of the Protestant, Catholic, Orthodox, Ethiopic, Syriac, and Samaritan Church*
- *Lost Books of the Bible: The Great Rejected Texts*
- *The Book of Jasher*
- *Book of Enoch, Jubilees, Jasher & The Book of Giants: The Complete Scriptures of Nephilim & Fallen Angels*
- *The Books of Enoch and The Book of Giants (featuring 1, 2, and 3 Enoch with the Aramaic and Manichean Giants texts)*
- *The Book of Jubilees: The Little Genesis, The Apocalypse of Moses*
- *The First and Second Books of Adam and Eve*
- *The Pentautech: The 5 Books of Moses*
- *The War Scroll: The War of the Sons of Light Against the Sons of Darkness*
- *The Kebra Nagast : The Glory of the Kings*
- *The Book of the Bee: The Syriac Text*
- *The Holy Piby: The Blackman's Bible*
- *The Gospel of Nicodemus, the Acts of Pilate and the Harrowing of Hell*
- *The Books of Jasher*

www.ingramcontent.com/pod-product-compliance
Lightning Source LLC
Chambersburg PA
CBHW071515040426
42444CB00008B/1656